I Use My Skills!

Knowing Your Strengths

Tana Hensley

SOCIAL AND EMOTIONAL LEARNING FOR THE REAL WORLD™

Rosen Classroom™

Everyone is different.
We have different strengths.

I have special skills.
They are my strengths!

I am good at drawing.
I can draw anything!

Drawing is my special skill.
I draw pictures for my friends.

Sara is good at baking.
She makes cupcakes!

Sara is good at sharing, too.
She shares cupcakes with our class!

Dave is good at singing.
That is his skill!

He makes people smile
when he sings.

It is our teacher's birthday.
We use our skills together!

I draw a card.
Sara bakes a cake.
Dave sings "Happy Birthday"!

Words to Know

card

cupcake

picture